# Welcome The Rain

Choosing to See Beyond
Life's Storm

Michelle Sedas

FOREWORD BY ERIC HARVEY

# WALKTHETALK.COM

## Resources for Personal and Professional Success

Helping Individuals and Organizations Achieve Success
Through Values-Based Practices

## Welcome The Rain

The WALK THE TALK Company
1100 Parker Square, Suite 250
Flower Mound, Texas  75028
972.899.8300

WALK THE TALK books may be purchased for educational, business, or sales promotion use.

WALK THE TALK® and The WALK THE TALK® Company are registered trademarks of Performance Systems Corporation.

WELCOME THE RAIN™ is a trademark of Michelle Sedas.

Printed in the United States of America
10  9  8  7  6  5  4  3  2  1

Designed by Sandra Beddow
Printed by Branch-Smith

ISBN-13:   978-1-885228-87-1

90000

9 781885 228871

*Dedicated to*
*Hebert, Diego, and Isabella –*
*the greatest blessings in my life*

*WELCOME THE RAIN*

# Table of Contents

6    Foreword by Eric Harvey

10    Prologue

18    Introduction

24    Welcome . . .

26    Welcome Adversity

32    Welcome Chaos

38    Welcome Controversy

44    Welcome Pain

50    Welcome Disaster

56    Welcome Stress

62    Welcome Second Place

68    Welcome Inconvenience

74    Welcome The Search

80    Welcome Delay

86    Welcome Mistakes

92    Welcome The Challenge

98    Welcome The Unexpected

102    Think About Such Things

112    Welcome The Rain

116    Epilogue: My Rain. My Story.

# *Foreword*

*by Eric Harvey*

*W*elcome The Rain is a reminder to me, and a gift to us all, that we've been given the opportunity to choose our attitudes. This certainly doesn't mean any of us will avoid the trials and tribulations of life, but it does mean that every one of us can decide whether they become debilitating or developmental.

On a rainy morning in 1969, two days after I was married, I was sitting in the Armed Services Induction Station in Newark, New Jersey, having just been drafted into the Army during the height of the Vietnam War. There is no doubt that I was confused, scared, and had considerable anxiety about my future.

During the many hurry-up-and-wait segments of that day, I struck up a conversation with a kid from North Jersey. Between our conversations, I noticed he was writing in a small spiral notebook. Finally, I asked him something like, "Hey, you writing a book or what?"

He said, "No, I'm just trying to write down all of the good things about being drafted in the army."

I remembered being both surprised and intrigued. At this point, I tuned out his words and my thoughts turned inward. *Good things? This guy is making a list of good things? The only things I can think about are being separated from my wife, spending time in harm's way, facing an uncertain future*…When I mentally rejoined our conversation, he was mid-sentence, rattling off a list of his good things. "…a chance to serve my country, an opportunity to visit places I've never seen, being able to pay for my college with the GI bill…"

I was truly amazed about how he could redefine and repurpose this scary and negative situation into something profoundly positive. When I first read Michelle Sedas' *Welcome The Rain*, this memorable experience flooded back to my mind. I remembered how, almost forty years ago, this North Jersey kid had captured the essence of welcoming his rain.

After my time in the army, I did come home safe and sound, was proud to serve my country, visited places I had never been, and went to college paid for by the GI bill. Having the right mindset makes all the difference in the world.

*T*hirty years ago I, along with a few colleagues, laid the cornerstone for a human resource consulting and training organization specializing in values-based business practices. As road warriors, we were constantly in front of our clients, building skills, changing attitudes, and improving behaviors of individuals and organizations. Eventually, I coauthored a book entitled *WALK THE TALK … And Get The Results You Want*, which became a bestseller. We were extremely delighted with the success of this product so our company expanded by developing a publishing division.

Five years ago, Michelle Sedas joined our WALK THE TALK team to help us enhance our customer service department, but we quickly discovered she had extraordinary writing and editing talent. As one of our editors, Michelle demonstrated her talent by helping to turn many manuscripts into successful final books. Last winter, Michelle asked if I would be willing to read a manuscript that she had written herself and had been working on for the past few years. Intrigued, I told her I would read it the following weekend and get back with her on Monday with my reactions. I have to admit that I was a bit concerned with my commitment because I value my professional relationship with her, and I had my fingers crossed that she had produced a book that would be worthy of some sort of positive feedback.

I distinctly remember sitting down on a Saturday afternoon by my fireplace with a stack of six manuscripts to read, including Michelle's. As I would finish one and write down my margin notes and comments, I would restack the group. For some reason I noticed that I kept putting Michelle's at the bottom of my stack. To this day, I'm not sure whether or not I was subconsciously doing it for some scientific reason or just postponing the potential possibility that I would have to give her negative feedback about her "baby" on Monday.

As I started to read *Welcome The Rain*, I began realizing that Michelle not only had written a wonderfully worded and designed book, but also captured one of life's secrets in a clear and compelling fashion. When I finished the book, I noticed I had made no margin notes as I was reading, and my mood was contemplative – not so much about what I had just read, but more about what I had just learned and absorbed.

***Welcome The Rain*** is one of the top ten most powerful books I've ever read. More importantly, it has given me, as I hope it will you, life lessons that will go beyond the mere enjoyment of reading this book.

WELCOME THE RAIN

*Prologue*

*O*minous charcoal clouds
roll in from the east.
Blackness envelopes the sky.
What begins as a single drop
develops into a steady, rhythmic

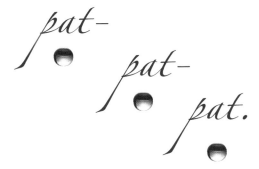

*pat–*

*pat–*

*pat.*

*Suddenly,*

the skies open up
and a downpour of rain
saturates the thirsty earth...

# A businessman

drives to a meeting and sees the
raindrops splatter onto the windshield
of his recently washed car. Disgusted,
he rolls his eyes and, with clenched fist,
lets out a long sigh. Angry that traffic will
be congested and upset that
he may get his new Italian leather
shoes wet, he thinks:

*Outside of town,*

a farmer scans the horizon. Upon seeing the first raindrops fall to the earth, he calls out to the rest of his family in celebration. After many weeks of drought, his crop will at last receive the sustenance that it so deeply needs. He thinks:

*What a*

*wonderful turn*

*of events!*

*We are so*

*blessed!*

WELCOME THE RAIN

*Introduction*

$\mathcal{I}$t is certain that in every life rain will come. The rain represents the situations, sensations, conditions, and events that we try to avoid: adversity, controversy, stress, pain, inconvenience, and delay. We do not intentionally seek out these tough challenges. We do not desire to face these difficulties. We do not want to weather these storms. When the rain does come, it is our human nature to allow these times to get the best of us, to overwhelm us, to cause us to sink.

However, when we can appreciate these challenging times and respect their value in our lives, we come to a place of contentment. When we can see beyond our current difficulties and realize that these challenging times will make us stronger, allow us to grow, and give us a deep admiration for the blessings that life grants us, we truly open our eyes with optimism. And when we understand that ultimately we are in control of the way we respond to and think about life's events, that only we have the ability to choose the thoughts that enter our minds, we discover absolute freedom. No longer are our attitudes tied to what happens to us. Such hope is there in knowing that when faced with any type of circumstance, the truth remains, after all, that

*life is what we choose to make of it.*

*When your rain comes...*

will you choose to be the businessman, upset at how the storm has inconvenienced you? Or will you choose to be the farmer who knows that while rain has the potential to be destructive it also brings growth and new life?

It is my wish that after reading this book, you will never see *the rain* the same way again. When the first drops fall, may you be reminded to think differently about facing life's obstacles. May you choose to see beyond life's storms, to uncover the blessings that the rain brings, and during all of life's twists and turns, may you always *choose to...*

*Welcome The Rain.*

*Man's mind stretched to a new idea
never goes back to its original dimensions.*

*~ Oliver Wendell Holmes, Jr. ~*

WELCOME THE RAIN

*It's not the way
the wind blows,
it's how you set
your sails.*

~ Unknown ~

*WELCOME THE RAIN*

*Welcome...*

# Welcome Adversity

Adversity has the effect of
eliciting talents,
which in prosperous circumstances
would have lain dormant.

~ *Horace* ~

*E*rik Weihenmayer has climbed to the highest peaks on each of the seven continents. On September 5, 2002, the day of his seventh summit, he joined a group of less than 100 people to ever do the same. It is his incredible inner strength that has allowed him to withstand the powerful elements of nature: roaring winds, ice blizzards, and oxygen depletion. Erik, the ultimate athlete, also runs marathons, is a long distance cyclist, and paraglides. One last note about Erik: He is blind.

*Conquering any difficulty always gives one*

*a secret joy, for it means pushing back a*

*boundary-line and adding to one's liberty.*

*~ Henri Frédéric Amiel ~*

As the first blind man to summit Mt. Everest, Erik has shattered the world's perceptions of blind people. And while he says, "I don't climb mountains to prove blind people can climb mountains; I climb mountains because I love it," clearly, he has shown it's not about what you have, it's what you *do* with what you're given.

The human spirit can be unconquerable. We have the ability to push ourselves beyond the seemingly rigid laws of nature. By *Welcoming Adversity* and not becoming overwhelmed by physical limitations, this man has shown us that one's *state of mind is everything*.

*He is a wise man who does not grieve for the things which he has not, but rejoices for those which he has.*

*~ Epictetus ~*

Thought is the

*sculptor*

who can create the person

you want to be.

~ *Henry David Thoreau* ~

# Welcome Chaos

*Chaos is a friend of mine.*

~ Bob Dylan ~

*D*uring a recent stormy afternoon I was at home with my two children when the power went out. Taking advantage of the last few moments of the natural light streaming through the windows, I gathered supplies: candles, matches, flashlights, and emergency lamps. After an hour, the electricity came back on and we greeted it with cheers, hoots, and hollers. Ten minutes later, our electricity went out again. This cycle continued for the next hour and a half: *Hooray!* when the lights came on and *Oh, not again!* when the lights went out. While I was semi-annoyed but still having fun with all of the cheering and booing, I saw genuine disappointment on my three-year-old son's face every time the lights went out. I then realized the absurdity of it all: I was writing a book on *perspective* and *not letting external events dictate your attitude* and I was teaching my son to be happy when the electricity was on and to be frustrated when the lights went off.

It was then that I tried a new tactic. We began to read books by the light of our battery powered lamps. Almost immediately, the emotions in our house changed from an up-and-down rollercoaster ride to an even-keeled quiet serenity. The lights continued to flicker and yet we continued to read…

*In moments of chaos,* we can become swept away with emotion, or we can choose to become our own stabilizing factor. When we force ourselves to become steady and firmly grounded in moments of chaos, we can then find unwavering peace.

## Chaos often breeds life, when order breeds habit.

*~ Henry Brooks Adams ~*

It's better to

light a candle

than to curse

the darkness.

*~ Chinese Proverb ~*

# Welcome
# Controversy

The ultimate measure of a man

is not where he stands in moments

of comfort and convenience,

but where he stands at times

of challenge and controversy.

~ *Martin Luther King, Jr.* ~

Life in Utopia is peaceful, gentle, kind, and full of harmony.

Everyone thinks the same way and holds the same beliefs.

Dissention is non-existent and agreement runs rampant.

*We do not live in Utopia.*

Unfortunately, *our world will never be perfect*. This real-life existence is full of controversy and challenges. And while controversial times cause tension, keep us in a state of anxiety, and encourage contention, could they actually be blessings in disguise?

The truth is that our finest moments are most likely to occur when we are feeling deeply uncomfortable, unhappy, or unfulfilled. For it is only in such moments, propelled by our discomfort, that we are likely to step out of our ruts and start searching for different ways or truer answers.

~ M. Scott Peck ~

*Moments of controversy* can raise public awareness about social injustices. What began as an act of defiance, some consider to be the beginning of the modern day civil rights movement. On December 1, 1955, Rosa Parks refused to give up her bus seat to a white passenger and was then arrested and tried for civil disobedience. This event sparked the Montgomery Bus Boycott and introduced the nation to Martin Luther King, Jr. Her controversial decision to break a city ordinance eventually led to the end of legal segregation in America.

Differing views, opinions, and beliefs add texture and color to the world's tapestry. Choose to stand (or sit!), speak up, and act out for what you believe. Controversial times, while difficult to weather, can change the world.

As we sail through life,
don't avoid rough waters,
sail on because calm waters
won't make a skillful sailor.

~ *Unknown* ~

# Welcome
## Pain

God whispers to us in our pleasures,

speaks to us in our conscience,

but shouts in our pains:

it is His megaphone to rouse

a deaf world.

*~ C. S. Lewis ~*

*D*r. Paul Brand was an orthopedic surgeon who dedicated his life to understanding leprosy. Through his research, he found that, contrary to popular belief, the disease leprosy itself does not cause the flesh to deteriorate. The disease actually keeps the person from feeling pain. It is this cessation of pain that causes the patient to become deformed. A person with leprosy may place his hand on a hot stove and, by not feeling pain, may burn away part of his hand. Another patient may cut his leg without noticing and, left untreated, the severe infection may cause part of the leg to be amputated. Dr. Brand's research shows us that the physical sensation of pain is not only beneficial, but is crucial for survival.

Emotional pain also has its place in our lives. When you find yourself feeling pain, be reassured that pain is there to protect and preserve us. By removing our hand from the hot stove or by remembering the pain we felt when we hurt our loved ones, pain allows us to change our ways.

*We could never learn to be brave and*
*patient if there were only joy in the world.*

*~ Helen Keller ~*

Relaxing with his friends, a man enjoys a few beers. He's just enjoying the moment and does it really hurt anyone if he needs to escape a little? After his friends notice a pattern of slurred speech while out playing golf, they make innocent remarks. To which he replies,

*"I just needed to take the edge off. This week at the office was brutal."*

For the second time this week, his spouse hears the wine bottles clank when he takes out the trash. Sensing subtle changes in his behavior, she finally admits to herself that there is a problem. When she asks him about his drinking, he says,

*"It was a tough week. I just needed to relax."*

At a business dinner with clients, he has wine to calm his nerves. Landing this huge account will help to ease his money worries. On the way home, he gets a ticket for driving under the influence. He says,

*"Officer, I promise it was just this one time."*

One evening, angry over a minor disagreement with his wife, he goes into a drunken rage. The dishes that he throws against the wall shatter into pieces. He hears a gasp and slowly turns his head. Looking across the room into the shadows beneath the stairs, he sees fear in his twelve-year-old son's face. This sobering image pierces his heart and finally causes him to say,

*"I need help."*

Life begins on the

other side of despair.

~ *Jean-Paul Sartre* ~

Welcome
Disaster

WELCOME THE RAIN

I always tried to
turn every disaster
into an opportunity.

*~ John D. Rockefeller ~*

*F*ire is one of nature's most destructive elements. In order to harness this powerful force, firefighters use a technique called *prescribed burn* where they systematically and intentionally set a fire to clear out large accumulations of flammable material. This *prescribed burn* is one of the most effective methods to prevent wildfires. Another technique, called *backfire*, is used when wildfires are burning out of control. In this case, the firefighters will burn areas ahead of the fire in order to cut off the fuel source. While the harmful effects of wildfire can be catastrophic, using this powerful element, at the right intensity, at the right time, and under the right circumstance prevents great loss. This intentional use of fire, purposefully causing disaster, can eliminate much destruction from occurring.

*Nothing in life is to be feared.*

*It is only to be understood.*

~ Marie Curie ~

*What we see depends mainly on what we look for.*

~ John Lubbock ~

We can learn from our leaders of the past. Thomas Edison's great optimism gives us a quintessential example of *Welcoming Disaster*:

On a December night in 1914, fire broke out in the film room of Thomas Edison's laboratory. As his assets were going up in smoke, it would seem that this sixty-seven-year-old man's spirit would certainly be crushed.

Instead, he saw the fire and shouted to his son, "Where's Mom? Go get her! Tell her to get her friends! They'll never see a fire like this again!" Later, he said,

> *"You can always make capital out of disaster.*
> *We've just cleared out a bunch of old rubbish.*
> *We'll build bigger and better on the ruins."*

Thomas Edison could not control the circumstances. Rather than being heart-broken to see his life's work go up in flames, he chose to welcome the opportunity to start over. Edison, known for his overwhelming optimism, is an inspiration for us today.

An optimist is

the human

personification

of spring.

~ *Susan J. Bissonette* ~

# Welcome
# Stress

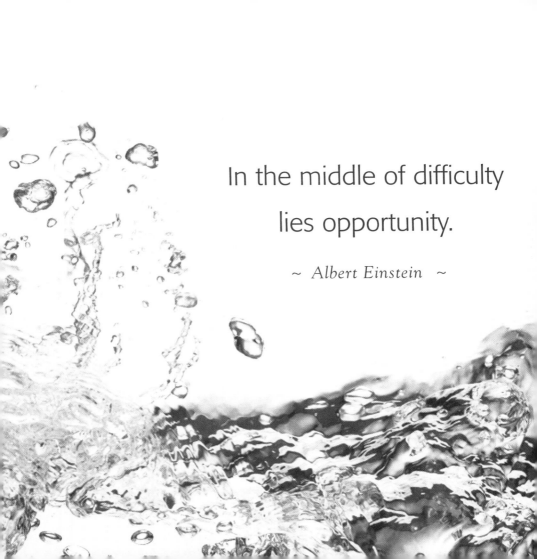

In the middle of difficulty

lies opportunity.

*~ Albert Einstein ~*

*Y*our heart begins to race; you can feel the rush of adrenaline. As your palms perspire and your mouth goes dry, you feel the butterflies in your stomach. You are keenly aware that this is the moment you have prepared for. You gaze upon the crowd and see that all eyes are watching you with anticipation. After a deep inhale and a slow exhale you begin…

The executive who is sharp, mentally focused, and able to deliver a killer presentation and the athlete who performs better in competition than in practice can tell you that stress can be used to one's advantage. On the field or in the boardroom, stress can become our ally. Moderate levels of stress help us get out of bed in the morning, give us motivation, and supply us with the drive to complete a difficult task. Stress can provide us with inspiration for performing our jobs well. In fact, a lack or inadequate amount of stress can cause a person to feel depressed.

Cavemen depended upon these physical reactions to stress in order to survive. When confronted with anything that posed a threat, the body's reaction to stress allowed the cavemen to be more alert, focused, and ready to fight or flee. It is this survival response that we still feel today when faced with stressful situations.

*Adopting the right attitude can convert a*
*negative stress into a positive one.*

~ Hans Selye ~

Stress can be useful in numerous ways. Engineers test a material's strength by applying stress. During testing, the engineer is able to find the material's weak spots. These weak spots can then be reinforced to make the material stronger. Similarly, cardiac stress tests measure the heart's blood flow during exercise (stress) as opposed to during periods of rest. Doctors are able to detect some types of heart disease—weak spots in the heart muscle—after a patient undergoes stress testing. In nature, continual wind on a tree can cause it to become very strong. This ever-present stress forces the tree to stay grounded, dig deep, and remain firmly planted in the ground.

Whether it is just enough to keep us motivated, or strong enough to expose our weak spots, stress can give us opportunities to improve ourselves.

Problems are to the mind

what exercise is

to the muscles,

they toughen

and make strong.

~ *Norman Vincent Peale* ~

# Welcome
## Second Place

*Our greatest glory is not*

*in never falling,*

*but in rising every time we fall.*

~ Confucius ~

We all dream of being the best, the champion, the gold-medal winner. Recognition, pride, a sense of accomplishment, and elation come with winning. It's easy to be a winner. We all want to win, and yet, do we really grow and learn when we win? The real challenge comes when we lose.

When I was in the third grade, I competed in the school spelling bee. Standing in front of the audience in the auditorium, I can still see the lights, remember the anxiety, hear my voice quiver as I spelled each word aloud. I have no idea what my first two words were. But, I will never forget how to spell *obituary*. It was my last and final word. As I sat watching the spelling bee continue on without me, this word began to permanently etch itself into my memory. While it is fun and exciting to be a winner, real character is built when we suffer defeat. When we lose, we learn.

# How you think when you lose determines how long it will be until you win.

~ G. K. Chesterton ~

On June 18, 1941, boxer Billy Conn put his Light-Heavyweight title on the line to fight Heavyweight champion Joe Lewis in what some consider one of the greatest fights of the century. Weighing 169 ½ pounds against Joe's 200 pounds, Billy was the 4 to 1 underdog. A determined fighter, Billy outboxed his larger opponent and was ahead on the scorecards through 12 rounds. It was in round 13 that Joe Lewis knocked out Billy Conn. Although Billy lost, he gained respect for his determination. The greatest victories are not evidenced by the final score, they are seen in the players' drive and persistence.

The greatest part of

our happiness

depends on our dispositions,

not our circumstances.

~ *Martha Washington* ~

Welcome
Inconvenience

WELCOME THE RAIN

An inconvenience

is only an adventure

wrongly considered.

~ G. K. Chesterton ~

At the beginning of 1996, Lance Armstrong was the number one ranked cyclist in the world. And by early October, Lance had been diagnosed with testicular cancer, which had spread to his lungs and brain. He was given a less than fifty percent chance of survival. With the help of specialists and chemotherapy, he fought the illness and won. Lance then went on to win seven Tour de France titles.

Despite the pain and suffering, Lance Armstrong considers cancer to be the *best thing* that ever happened to him. In his book, *It's Not About the Bike*, he said, "I don't know why I got the illness, but it did wonders for me, and I wouldn't want to walk away from it. Why would I want to change even for a day, the most important and shaping event in my life?"

*Where there is no struggle,*

*there is no strength.*

~ Oprah Winfrey ~

I would certainly consider cancer to be the most inconvenient thing that could ever happen to me. But by *Welcoming Inconvenience*, Lance says, "When I was sick, I saw more beauty and triumph and truth in a single day than I ever did in a bike race." If you cannot change what happens, then for your happiness, you must *change your mindset*. The knowledge that life's events can be blessings in disguise can help us weather the toughest storms.

I'm not afraid of storms,
for I'm learning how to
sail my ship.

~ *Louisa May Alcott* ~

# Welcome The Search

WELCOME THE RAIN

Only as high as I reach can I grow,

only as far as I seek can I go,

only as deep as I look can I see,

only as much as I dream can I be.

~ *Karen Ravn* ~

While on vacation in Mexico, my husband and I met a man. He was my age, also had a preschool-aged child, played the same sport as a youth that paid my father's way through college (baseball), smiled easily and welcomed conversation; yet it seemed as if that is where our similarities ended.

Within the first two minutes of speaking with him, we found out that he was from Cuba. While he spoke timidly at first, he warmed up to our questions about his country, his life, and his experiences. Over the next *two hours* we learned so much about a country that is only ninety miles from Florida, but a world away with respect to culture and liberty. Once he began speaking, it was as if a reservoir of feelings had broken loose. It was clear that he was delighted to have people to share his experiences with. With passion and conviction he spoke about his homeland: a beautiful country rich in history and yet had many citizens who were struggling.

This Cuban cigar roller, sitting at his table selling his *puros*, spoke mostly of a universal theme: freedom and how the denial of this freedom would force a person to go to great lengths to obtain it. He told us of conversations he had with people from other countries who worked in the same resort.

"They will complain and say, 'I only made forty dollars today.' Forty dollars! I remember once back home when I didn't make forty dollars in a whole year. And in my homeland, we do not say, 'What kind of car do you have?' rather it's, 'Wow! You have a car!' To the people who complain I want to say, *'Do you not know? This place is wonderful! This is the good life.'*"

While searching for freedom and meaning, this man has found his dream life in an unfamiliar land, in a place where others have found fault.

The next time you are tempted to complain about the terrible thing that happened at work, or the crazy way your children behaved today, or the unkind way some-one cut you off on the freeway (while you were driving your own car!), remember that there is always someone else out there who would say, *"Do you not know? Your life is a dream!"*

*Search for the dream
in the life you are already living.*

Everything can be taken from a man but one thing: the last of the human freedoms — to choose one's attitude in any given set of circumstances, to choose one's own way.

~ *Viktor Frankl* ~

Since we cannot

change reality,

let us change the eyes

which see reality.

~ *Nikos Kazantzakis* ~

# Welcome Delay

*Adopt the pace of nature:*

*her secret is patience.*

~ Ralph Waldo Emerson ~

*I*n my childhood, a favorite vacation destination for my family was Hot Springs, Arkansas. This drive took five hours when my father was with us, but somehow managed to evolve into a much longer trip when it was just the girls. Oh how we loved to stop and shop.

One year, my mother, grandmother, Aunt Marelen, and I were on our drive back home when it began to rain. Because of the intensity of the storm, we decided it would be a good time to take a pit stop: allowing us to refuel our car and our bodies. I quickly found my snacks and was ready to get back on the road. After all, this was a "girl trip" and we were approaching hour *seven* of our "five-hour trip" back home. As I was waiting in line to buy my snacks, I was becoming increasingly anxious. The lady behind the counter was taking forever. I looked at my watch and was so annoyed that I had to stand in that line for *ten whole minutes*. It was ridiculous. *I wish we could get out of here and be on our way*, I thought. *Stop being friendly to your customers, just ring me up*, I wanted to tell the clerk.

Back in the car, a couple of miles down the road, we came across an eerie scene: Cars were parked along the side of the road. People, who had been huddled in the small wedge between an overpass and the embankment, were beginning to climb back down the hill to their cars. Children, from a daycare, were among this group.

We slowed to a snail's pace as all lanes of traffic merged onto the shoulder of the road. We called out of our window at the people going back to their cars, "What happened?"

A man replied, "The radio told everyone to take cover immediately. A fierce storm came through. Blew these huge trees down. All of us took cover under the bridge. These trees fell right down on the road *a little over ten minutes ago.*"

*Ten minutes in line. A little while later we arrived at the scene.*

I was speechless. As the hairs on my arm stood on end, I bowed my head. *Thank you* for the kind, too talkative cashier. *Thank you* for not letting me get my wish to get out of there. *Thank you* for our ten-minute delay.

From our perspective, we may not be able to see the whole picture. Often, we do not know what lies just down the road. *Welcome Delay* for it may be exactly what we need at the time.

> *To him that waits all things reveal themselves,*
> *provided that he has the courage not to deny,*
> *in the darkness, what he has seen in the light.*

~ Coventry Patmore ~

You can complain because

roses have thorns,

or you can rejoice because

thorns have roses.

*~ Ziggy ~*

# Welcome
# Mistakes

The only real mistake is

the one from which we

learn nothing.

~ *John Powell* ~

*M*y grandmother was born in a small West Texas farming town on August 26th, 1929, two months and three days before Black Tuesday, the Stock Market crash that started the Great Depression. As the youngest daughter of sharecroppers, who earned their living by picking cotton, she knew the meaning of barely getting by. Times were tough and she learned to never waste anything.

Her Uncle Jess was a compassionate man who always treated her with kindness. Each time she would visit him, she always left with the same feeling: *I am special*. After all, she was the *only person* who was allowed to drink from his special pink drinking glass. One day, she took the pink glass out to the water cooler, a special room that stored and cooled the water generated from the windmill. Out in the water cooler, she dropped *the* glass. Looking down at the hundreds of glass fragments, she began to cry. She had been entrusted with this special glass and now it was broken.

Her crying was interrupted when she heard Uncle Jess call out, "Ruby Nell, I was thinking. I'm tired of that silly old pink glass. Would you please break it for me?" She ran back to him calling out, with the enthusiasm that only a six-year-old can summon, *"I did it, Uncle Jess! I did it!"*

The way we choose to respond when others make mistakes can cause them to feel ashamed or can allow them to remember our kindness and share our stories with future generations. We choose our legacy that gets passed down to others.

I expect to pass through this life but once.
Therefore, if there be any kindness I can show,
or any good thing I can do for another human being,
let me do it now,
for I shall not pass this way again.

*~ William Penn ~*

What we call

the secret of happiness

is no more a secret

than our willingness

to choose life.

~ *Leo Buscaglia* ~

Welcome The Challenge

The harder the conflict,

the more glorious the triumph.

What we obtain too cheap,

we esteem too lightly;

it is dearness only that

gives everything its value.

I love the man that can smile in trouble,

that can gather strength from distress

and grow brave by reflection.

~ *Thomas Paine* ~

*M*y husband grew up in Mexico in a well-respected, educated, and loving family. When he was a junior in high school, his family attended a cousin's wedding in College Station, Texas. During this trip, the family car drove by the campus of Texas A&M University. After only seeing the campus from the car window, it was then that he knew *this* was where he wanted to go to college. There was only one problem: He didn't speak English.

The following fall, during his senior year of high school, he took English night classes. Finally, the time had come for him to take the English entrance exam: a passing grade was a prerequisite for attending universities in the U.S. The results came back: *fail.* Then, after months of working with a private English tutor, he took the entrance exam again. Again the results: *fail.* The summer following his high school graduation, he attended a summer school at a university in Texas. He took the exam two times during this summer. Again: *fail* and *fail.*

Finally, he went to a semester-long English program. At the end of the course, it was time again to take the dreaded English entrance exam. Since the exam wasn't offered locally when he needed to take it, he endured a three-hour bus trip and a taxi ride to get to the exam site in order to sit for the three-hour exam.

This time the results came back: *PASS!*

With perseverance and unwavering determination, my husband eventually went on to earn his Bachelor of Science degree from Texas A&M. What a message to send to our children. Had he given up, after the first, second, or even fourth time of taking the exam, we never would have met.

When I asked him how he did it, he replied, "Go after what you want. Sometimes, it's the challenge of something that makes you want it even more." And as he said, "Then, there just comes a time when you've got to *'swim or sink.'*"

Try, try, try, try, and try again until you finally succeed.

Accept the challenges so that you may
feel the exhilaration of victory.

~ *General George S. Patton* ~

The greatest power that
a person possesses is
the power to choose.

~ *J. Martin Kohe* ~

Welcome

The Unexpected

*Joy is not in things;*
*it is in us.*

~ Richard Wagner ~

*I* was seven years old and my mother and I were out running errands. In Texas, weather is sporadic, unpredictable, ever-changing. As my mother drove, the storm clouds opened up and the noon sky became a menacing black. Large raindrops began to splatter onto the windshield. When she was eventually unable to see, my mother pulled off onto the side of the road. Soon, small, pea-sized hail was falling. When the large quarter-sized hail stones pummeled the top of our car, I was in tears.

Smiling joyfully, my mother told me that if the hail damaged our car, we could get a new paint job. "Isn't this great? And if the hail *breaks* our wind-shield, we can get a new car!" The joy in my mother's face was contagious. Huddled in the back seat with a blanket over our heads, we listened as the hail fell. With each crash, we shrieked with delight. "Yea! A new car! Come on! We want more!"

As the hail intensified, so did our applause.

Clapping, screaming, smiling, hoping…

to protect her little girl from being afraid,

my mother, in a time of crisis…

*Welcomed The Rain.*

WELCOME THE RAIN

# Think About Such Things

Finally, brothers,

whatever is true, whatever is noble,

whatever is right,

whatever is lovely, whatever is admirable

—if anything is excellent

or praiseworthy—

think about such things.

~ *Philippians 4:8* ~

# Find Your Lifeboat

Many times, it is after the fact that we realize how *the rain* has shaped us. When we are in the midst of the storm, the idea that *the difficult times are what make us grow* sounds ridiculous. The concept of becoming better and stronger is elusive. During these times, it's okay to not move forward. Trying to stay above water may be all that we're capable of.

To keep from sinking, take your thoughts captive and *find your lifeboat*. Take a story from this book, current events, a mental image, an inspirational quote, whatever will serve as a reminder that others have survived terrible storms and have flourished. Even if it *seems* that nothing positive will ever come out of what happens, know that you will have gained empathy that will allow you to be sensitive to others in their times of need. To stay above water, find some idea that offers you hope and hold on to it.

The effects of holding on to hope can be amazing. In the movie *Cast Away*, Tom Hanks' character has been marooned on an island, alone, for four years. Back at home when he reflects upon that time and how he made it through he says:

"*I knew somehow that I had to stay alive. Somehow I had to keep breathing even though there was no reason to hope and all my logic said that I would never see this place again. So that's what I did. I stayed alive. I kept breathing….Then one day that logic was proven all wrong because the tide came in and gave me a sail and now here I am….I know what I have to do now, because we've got to keep breathing, because tomorrow the sun will rise. Who knows what the tide could bring.*"

*Hope is the feeling we have that the feeling we have is not permanent.*

~ Mignon McLaughlin ~

# My Lifeboat

I run. Not because I'm good at it. In fact, I look like a penguin and feel like an elephant when I run. My feet are flat, I'm knock-kneed, and I just plain look goofy. I run because of how it helps my thinking. The structure for this book came to me while running. During difficult runs when I feel I can run no farther, I slow my pace, look straight ahead, fix my eyes on a distant focal point, and remind myself that running is just

*one foot in front of the other.*

*Once you choose hope, anything's possible.*

~ *Christopher Reeve* ~

I scroll through mental images and decide that if the single mother can get her children to school and herself to work every day, then I can put one foot in front of the other. If my grandfather, after being partially paralyzed from his stroke, could keep his cheery disposition and never complain about his physical limitations, then I can put one foot in front of the other. And if our men and women in uniform all over the world can act with courage each and every day, then yes, *most certainly* I can just put one foot in front of the other. Whether facing a literal or figurative hill, focus on the task at hand. Remember that this storm will pass.

Do not become overwhelmed.
Instead, take it one step at a time...
and just put one foot in front of the other.

WELCOME THE RAIN

Choose to see

beyond life's storms...

because it is only after the rain

that you will find your rainbow.

WELCOME THE RAIN

# Welcome The Rain

# Welcome The Rain

*By Michelle Sedas*

As the first raindrops fall to the ground
A businessman lets out an angry sigh.
Knowing traffic will be slow he thinks,
*Why me? Why today? Just tell me why!*

Outside of town, a farmer scans the horizon
As the storm clouds begin to roll in.
With joy and celebration he calls out,
*We are blessed! At last, this drought will end!*

In every life storms will come:
Adversity, Inconvenience, or Pain.
Only we can choose how we will respond:
To be overwhelmed or to *Welcome The Rain.*

It's not about what happens to us.
It's what we think, internalize, and perceive.
It's not about the external events.
It's what we choose to believe.

Believe the difficult times help us grow.
They build character, strength, and wisdom.
Believe life's challenges can truly be blessings.
And with this understanding comes freedom...

For we're no longer at the mercy of the wind,
Being forcefully tossed around.
When we can see life through different eyes
The world's joys and beauties abound.

So as you continue on life's journey,
And feel the presence of rain's first dew,
Stand strong, be determined, remain focused.
And remember what is so true:

When we choose to see beyond life's storms
A new perspective we will gain
Since we will only find our rainbow
After we . . .

*Welcome The Rain*

WELCOME THE RAIN

# Epilogue

## My Rain. My Story.

As a twelve-year-old, I was hospitalized for depression. My desire to be perfect was crippling. Thirteen years later, when I was twenty-five, I found the world too mean and unjust and I felt that I had control over nothing. I was, again, hospitalized for depression. This time, however, I was not on the Pediatric Unit. The walls were not bright with painted clouds. We did not make collages of animals nor did we create macaroni pictures. This was real. This was frightening. And this was a place that I vowed I would never return to.

At a time when I found the world too painful to live in, I was awestruck by some terminally ill patients' insatiable hunger for life. The irony did not go unnoticed: I was physically healthy, yet found myself overwhelmed by the world. I wanted no part in it. On the other hand, many people possessed such strength and determination to fight their illnesses, while facing the possible reality that their lives may be taken away from them. I wanted to harness their internal passion and find my own hunger for life. I yearned to *want* to live…to find the world a place that I desired to stay in. But I had yet to find the key.

My battle with depression is my own personal rain. *This rain came, despite my best efforts to prevent it.* As heartbreaking as that time period was, I am thankful for it because it has given me a richer appreciation and understanding of life. Had I never felt such deep despair, I may have never searched so diligently for ways to overcome negative thinking. I may have never explored these topics with such intensity. And while my faith and relationship with God kept me afloat through the toughest of times, I believe that ultimately He used my depression to help me seek out the key to my happiness:

*It's not about what happens. It's about perspective.*
*I may not be able to change what takes place, but*
*I can always choose to change my thinking.*

*I* may not be the most organized, or the most outgoing; the most confident, or the most courageous. But through my journey, I have come to know certain things:

> *I will never be perfect. Our world will never be perfect. The rain will come, despite my best efforts to prevent it. Life is what you choose to make of it. And state of mind is everything. If you cannot change what happens, then for your happiness, you must change your mindset. In difficult times, remember that this storm will pass. To keep from sinking, find your lifeboat. Just put one foot in front of the other. Keep breathing. And know that tomorrow the sun will rise...*

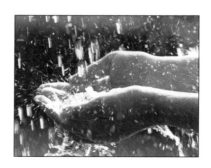

In my rainbow I have found
the sun shining on my face
as I jog along a Texas country road,
the peace of feeling that I am
unconditionally loved
despite my many faults,
the exhilaration of hearing my
newborn babies' first cries,
and the beauty of knowing that
tomorrow will come and that
I now welcome each new day
with open arms.

Enjoy the richness of life…
Rain and all,

# About The Publisher

Since 1977, The WALK THE TALK® Company has helped individuals and organizations, worldwide, achieve success through Values-Based Practices. Our goal is both simple and straightforward: to provide you and your organization with high-impact resources for your personal and professional success!

We specialize in…

- How-To Handbooks and Support Material
- Video Training Programs
- Inspirational Gift Books and Movies
- Do-It-Yourself Training Resources
- Motivational Newsletters
- 360° Feedback Processes
- The popular *212° the extra degree*™, *Start Right…Stay Right*, *Santa's Leadership Secrets*® product lines and much more!

To learn more:
Call: 1.888.822.9255
E-mail: info@walkthetalk.com
Visit: www.walkthetalk.com

# About The Author

Michelle Sedas is the editor of twenty-two books, including *WALK the TALK* gift book and *212° the extra degree* gift book. Other popular titles include *Start Right, Stay Right…Lead Right*; *Ouch! That Stereotype Hurts*; *What to Do When Conflict Happens*; *Leadership Courage*; and *Five Star Teamwork*.

*Welcome The Rain* is Michelle's first book. She received her bachelor's degree from Texas A&M University and is a member of Mensa International and Toastmasters International.

Michelle lives with her husband and two children, Diego and Isabella, in Texas. You can find her at www.michellesedas.com

# To order additional copies of *Welcome The Rain*, visit WalkTheTalk.com

Or, better yet, order the **Welcome The Rain** book and DVD Combo!

## The DVD contains 4 powerful resources:

- Welcome The Rain inspirational movie
- Welcome The Rain motivational screen saver
- Welcome The Rain printable poster
- Welcome The Rain personal action worksheet

### For a FREE preview of the inspirational movie, visit WalkTheTalk.com

*Quantity Discounts Available!*

## Introducing FREE online newsletters from WalkTheTalk.com

- **The Power of Inspiration** – Designed to uplift, inspire, and motivate you and the important people in your life.

- **Daily Motivation** – Powerful quotes to "kick start" your day.

- **Leadership Lessons** – Weekly tips to help you and your colleagues become more effective and respected leaders.

- *And More!*

WalkTheTalk.com newsletters are designed to motivate, inform, and inspire you to reach new levels of skills and confidence!

Visit WalkTheTalk.com to sign up and learn more!

*WELCOME THE RAIN*